ANIMALS OF THE CORAL REEF

Parrotfish

by Kate Moening

BLASTOFF! READERS
2

BELLWETHER MEDIA • MINNEAPOLIS, MN

Blastoff! Readers are carefully developed by literacy experts to build reading stamina and move students toward fluency by combining standards-based content with developmentally appropriate text.

Level 1 provides the most support through repetition of high-frequency words, light text, predictable sentence patterns, and strong visual support.

Level 2 offers early readers a bit more challenge through varied sentences, increased text load, and text-supportive special features.

Level 3 advances early-fluent readers toward fluency through increased text load, less reliance on photos, advancing concepts, longer sentences, and more complex special features.

★ **Blastoff! Universe**

Reading Level

Grade **K**

Grades **1–3**

Grade **4**

This edition first published in 2022 by Bellwether Media, Inc.

No part of this publication may be reproduced in whole or in part without written permission of the publisher. For information regarding permission, write to Bellwether Media, Inc., Attention: Permissions Department, 6012 Blue Circle Drive, Minnetonka, MN 55343.

Library of Congress Cataloging-in-Publication Data

Names: Moening, Kate, author.
Title: Parrotfish / by Kate Moening.
Description: Minneapolis, MN : Bellwether Media, [2022] | Series: Blastoff! readers : Animals of the coral reef | Includes bibliographical references and index. | Audience: Ages 5-8 | Audience: Grades 2-3 | Summary: "Relevant images match informative text in this introduction to parrotfish. Intended for students in kindergarten through third grade"--Provided by publisher.
Identifiers: LCCN 2021000532 (print) | LCCN 2021000533 (ebook) | ISBN 9781644875049 (library binding) | ISBN 9781648344121 (ebook)
Subjects: LCSH: Parrotfishes--Juvenile literature.
Classification: LCC QL638.S3 M64 2022 (print) | LCC QL638.S3 (ebook) | DDC 597/.7--dc23
LC record available at https://lccn.loc.gov/2021000532
LC ebook record available at https://lccn.loc.gov/2021000533

Editor: Elizabeth Neuenfeldt   Designer: Laura Sowers

Printed in the United States of America, North Mankato, MN.

Table of Contents

Life in the Coral Reef

rainbow parrotfish

Parrotfish are colorful fish.
They live in warm ocean waters.

They are found in coral reefs around the world.

Rainbow Parrotfish Range

N
W E
S

range = ☐

Young parrotfish are often brown. But adults have very colorful **scales**.

young and adult greenthroat parrotfish

bullethead parrotfish

This helps them hide in the colorful coral reef!

Parrotfish have strong teeth.
They look like a bird's beak.

bicolor parrotfish

teeth

Special Adaptations

rusty parrotfish

colorful scales

strong teeth

tail fin

These fish easily bite **corals** and rocks to get food! Teeth in their throats **grind** them down.

Parrotfish need
to swim fast to stay safe.
Their tail fins help!

Tail fins give parrotfish
a quick burst of speed.

← **tail fin**

**stoplight
parrotfish**

Rainbow Parrotfish Stats

Least Concern	Near Threatened	Vulnerable	Endangered	Critically Endangered	Extinct in the Wild	Extinct

conservation status: near threatened
life span: up to 16 years

Safety in Numbers

school of parrotfish

Many **predators** hunt in coral reefs.

Parrotfish often travel in **schools**. This helps them avoid danger.

Parrotfish sleep at night.
They hide under rocks or sand.

bubble of mucus
↓

Some make a bubble of **mucus** when they sleep. It hides their smell from predators!

Reef Caretakers

algae

↓

During the day, parrotfish look for food. These fish mostly eat **algae**.

They eat algae from rocks and corals. This helps corals stay clean!

Parrotfish Diet

algae

coral polyps

turtle grass

queen
parrotfish

Parrotfish cannot **digest** rocks
or corals. Their teeth grind rocks
and corals into sand. Then the
fish poop it out.

Most reef sand comes from parrotfish!

Parrotfish live well in the coral reef **biome**. They also help keep it clean.

steephead parrotfish

These fish are well **adapted** to their colorful home!

Glossary

adapted—well suited due to changes over a long period of time

algae—plants and plantlike living things; most kinds of algae grow in water.

biome—a large area with certain plants, animals, and weather

corals—the living ocean animals that build coral reefs

digest—to change food into a form that the body can use

grind—to crush or break something by rubbing it on a hard surface

mucus—a thick, slimy liquid that some parrotfish produce from their heads

predators—animals that hunt other animals for food

scales—small, stiff plates that cover the bodies of some animals

schools—groups of parrotfish

To Learn More

AT THE LIBRARY

Borgert-Spaniol, Megan. *Parrotfish: Coral Reef Cleaners*. Minneapolis, Minn.: Abdo Publishing, 2020.

Lawrence, Ellen. *Slime Sleepers: Parrotfish*. New York, N.Y.: Bearport Publishing, 2019.

Moening, Kate. *Angelfish*. Minneapolis, Minn.: Bellwether Media, 2022.

ON THE WEB

FACTSURFER

Factsurfer.com gives you a safe, fun way to find more information.

1. Go to www.factsurfer.com.

2. Enter "parrotfish" into the search box and click 🔍.

3. Select your book cover to see a list of related content.

Index